CW01151239

Original title:
Timber Tranquility

Copyright © 2025 Creative Arts Management OÜ
All rights reserved.

Author: Victor Mercer
ISBN HARDBACK: 978-1-80567-299-9
ISBN PAPERBACK: 978-1-80567-598-3

Serenity found Beneath the Sky

In the woods where squirrels dance,
And branches sway in silly prance,
A bear attempts to juggle pine,
While birds provide a comical line.

A raccoon wears a tiny hat,
As he tries to chat with a fat bat,
The trees stand tall, but giggle loud,
At antics of this woodland crowd.

A hedgehog with a tiny drum,
Beats a rhythm, oh so glum,
While rabbits hop in great delight,
Underneath the soft moonlight.

So let us frolic, laugh, and play,
In this quirky wood all day,
For peace resides where smiles bloom,
Beneath each leafy, funny room.

The Calm of Ancient Oaks

Beneath the leaves, squirrels dare,
Hiding acorns here and there.
The oaks stand tall in playful grace,
Losing hats at quite the pace.

A raccoon winks with mischief bright,
As he steals snacks under moonlight.
The wise old trees know all the jokes,
While birds gossip, flapping cloaks.

Tranquil Trails Through Timbered Realms

Along the trails, the shadows play,
While hikers trip and yell 'hooray!'
Nature chuckles, soft and clear,
At every stumble, every cheer.

A chipmunk scurries, quick and spry,
With nuts to stash; oh my, oh my!
Each step we take on forest's floor,
Might lead to laughter, who could ask for more?

The Soft Chorus of Leaves

The leaves all whisper jokes in trees,
While branches sway in gentle breeze.
They tease the wind, make it laugh out loud,
As clouds float by, feeling quite proud.

Each rustle's hint of secrets spilled,\nWhile ants march on,
their plans are willed.
A raccoon rolls with laughter bright,
While nature giggles through the night.

Harmony Under the Birch Canopy

Under the birch, the world is light,
With branches swaying, oh what a sight!
A deer prances, thinking she's quite sly,
As frogs croak tunes that make us sigh.

The sun peeks in, plays hide and seek,
While crickets chirp their nightly sneak.
In this realm, humor intertwines,
Where nature's quirks form lovely lines.

The Gentle Craft of Nature

The squirrels wear tiny hats, so bright,
Chasing each other with pure delight.
Leaves chuckle softly in the breeze,
While ants dance waltzes, if you please.

The owls hoot jokes with a wise old grin,
As woodpeckers play their wooden skin.
Even the mushrooms giggle and sway,
In this forest, silliness leads the way.

Whispers of the Woodland Spirit

The trees gossip about the clouds,
And the branches sway to cheerful crowds.
Bunnies bound with an air of flair,
While chipmunks juggle without a care.

A fox slips tripping on a wee twig,
His friends all laugh, "You're doing a jig!"
The brook giggles, splashing around,
In this forest, laughter knows no bound.

Echoes in the Green Sanctuary

In the glade, the breeze whispers tales,
Of dancing deer with their fluffy tails.
Frogs sing loud in a croaky choir,
While bees buzz tunes of sweet desire.

A turtle sneezes, causing a stir,
While fireflies giggle, a twinkling blur.
Even the shadows find ways to play,
In this sanctuary, joy lights the way.

The Calm of the Undergrowth

In the undergrowth, where secrets rest,
The critters compete for the silliest jest.
Mice trade laughs over crumbs of cheese,
While lizards lounge in the sun with ease.

A hedgehog rolls, makes quite a scene,
His spiky dance is fit for a queen!
The leaves applaud with a rustling cheer,
In this calm, all silly things appear.

Rustling Leaves

Behind the thicket, a joke is told,
By a wise old hedgehog, quite bold.
'Why did the beetle cross the street?'
To get to the flower, it's quite a feat!

An ant parade marches in line,
With tiny trumpets, they feel just fine.
They trumpeted tunes of old ballets,
Making the forest laugh in arrays.

Whispers of the Woodland

Squirrels chatter with cheeky delight,
While raccoons scheme in the soft moonlight.
A bear trips over his own two feet,
The laughter echoes, oh what a feat!

Trees giggle softly with leaves that sway,
As rabbits hop in their fanciful play.
A lonely owl hoots a tune out of tune,
Who knew that woods could hold such a boon?

A deer with a bowtie prances with glee,
While frogs host a party by the old pine tree.
The mushrooms tap-dance, a whimsical sight,
As fireflies boogie, lighting up the night.

Nature's jester, in every nook,
Bringing smiles with each funny look.
So join in the laughter, don't lag behind,
In this woodland wonder, true joy you'll find!

Beneath the Canopy of Peace

Beneath the leaves where shadows play,
A squirrel skids in a silly way.
He stops and blinks, looks quite bemused,
"I meant to fly!" he squeaks, confused!

There's laughter in the babbling brook,
As frogs in waistcoats read a book.
A turtle yawned and flipped on his back,
"Life is slow, and that's a fact!"

Tall trees are swaying, but not out of fear,
They're just grooving to tunes only they can hear.
With branches high like disco balls,
They host a party, bouncing off the walls!

The sun peeks in with a cheeky grin,
"Old log roll race? Let's begin!"
So close your eyes and let laughter reign,
In this peaceful place, joy's the main gain!

Serenity Amongst the Pines

Amidst the pines where the laughter roams,
A family of chipmunks call it home.
They argue about whose nuts are best,
As the wise old owl just takes a rest.

A hedgehog struts with a swagger so bold,
Wearing a hat made of leaves, quite old.
He waves at the passing hawks in flight,
"Come join my party! It's a real delight!"

The wind talks silly as it plays tag,
With the pinecones wagging, they laugh and swag.
Ballet of bugs on a delicate thread,
Twinkle toes tapping in sunshine ahead.

The sun sinks low, painting skies of gold,
A gentle breeze whispers stories untold.
With nature's comedy, life feels divine,
In this place among the ancient pines!

Echoes in the Grove

Echoes of giggles, soft and light,
As critters gather in pure delight.
A woodpecker knocks without a care,
"Who's messing up my style up there?"

Bunnies twist in a dance of flair,
Waving their tails with a cheeky air.
Then why not join in, leap and prance?
The woods become a stage for every chance!

Swaying ferns listen to gossip's flow,
While butterflies laugh at the lizard's show.
"It's not my fault!" the lizard cries,
A comical scene under azure skies.

As night descends, stars start to peek,
Nature's humor begins to speak.
In every corner, joy will thrive,
In the grove's warm heart, we come alive!

Twilight in the Green Haven

As daylight fades into night,
The squirrels dance with delight.
Chasing shadows, taking flight,
Beneath the stars, a silly sight.

The owls hoot like they've lost track,
While crickets sing a quirky crack.
Trees listen in, they're never slack,
With a rustle and a jovial quack.

A raccoon plots a midnight spree,
With acorns as his cup of tea.
He finds a toad, says, "Come with me!"
Together they laugh in harmony.

In this green haven, wild and free,
Where laughter grows on every tree.
The twilight whispers, "Let it be!"
As nature sings with glee, oh me!

Nature's Peaceful Reverie

A tree stump sits, a throne so grand,
The ants march by, a tiny band.
They wave their flags, with seedlings planned,
In nature's realm, all's unplanned.

A chipmunk juggles nuts like mad,
While the shadows play, it's quite a fad.
Squirrels laugh, 'Oh, don't be sad!'
As they join in, feeling glad.

Leaves giggle in the gentle breeze,
With funny sounds that aim to please.
A woodpecker's rhythm, if you please,
Makes the forest dance with ease.

So in this dream of green delight,
Where laughter rings from morn till night,
We find ourselves in nature's sight,
A joyful pause, a silly bite!

Gentle Whispers of the Foliage

The leaves converse in funny tones,
With secrets shared in hushed drones.
A squirrel drops nuts, hears wild moans,
As laughter echoes off their homes.

A butterfly flits, wears a grin,
While grasshoppers join in the din.
"Let's hop and skip, let fun begin!"
They chant aloud with zestful sin.

A wise old tortoise takes a nap,
Dreaming of leaves, in magical wrap.
But then he wakes—oh, what a trap!
Caught in a web of laughter's flap.

The foliage chuckles, what a scene,
In the shaded spots, oh so green.
Nature's gentle whims are keen,
Creating moments, bright and clean!

Arbor's Embrace

In the arms of trees, a jolly crew,
Bark is thick, but so are they too.
Cackling over a funny brew,
Nature's party, just me and you.

A hedgehog spins, a dance so fine,
While rabbits hop, and squirrels dine.
"A buffet of nuts, all around us, divine!"
They laugh and jump, feeling the sunshine.

The mossy carpet fills with cheer,
As gnomes play hide and seek, oh dear.
"Don't peek, don't peek!" they shout with fear,
As laughter bursts from ear to ear.

In this embrace of leafy fun,
Where every joy shines like the sun,
Life's silly rhythms weigh a ton,
But in the end, it's all just one!

Shades of Peace in the Pines

In a grove where squirrels conspire,
Chirping songs of their great empire.
A raccoon once tried to climb a tree,
But ended up stuck, laughing with glee.

Birds debate over best nesting spots,
While chipmunks stash unguarded pots.
Leaves giggle as the wind takes a spin,
Nature's joke is where chaos begins.

Whispers of breeze tickle the air,
As trees dance with a flair quite rare.
Mama bear grumbles, 'Where's my snack?'
As baby bears chase, silly and slack.

So come join this jovial scene today,
Where laughter echoes without delay.
In every shadow and bright sunbeam,
Nature's chuckles are always a dream.

Beneath the Boughs of Serenity

Under branches, a picnic unfolds,
With sandwiches and stories untold.
Ants unexpectedly join the feast,
While owls roll their eyes at the least.

Toadstools wear caps in vibrant hues,
As frogs debate what flavor to choose.
The sun peeks through, giving a wink,
While squirrels prod each other to think.

Daisies laugh, swaying in delight,
As butterflies dance in their light flight.
A whispered breeze tells a quaint joke,
The trees chuckle, giving a poke.

So gather beneath this canopy bright,
Where trees and laughter feel just right.
Nature's comedy is quite the affair,
Every moment shared is beyond compare.

The Sigh of the Forest Floor

Leaves rustle soft like whispers of cheer,
While mushrooms pop up, more than a few here.
A fox trips over roots with a yelp,
As the whole forest snickers, not one stealth.

Beneath the shade where the wild things play,
A beaver hums as he gnaws all day.
The chipmunks hold a talent show grand,
With acorns as props, it's totally planned.

Elder trees tell tales of the past,
While young saplings drift in bliss, unsurpassed.
The forest floor sighs with glee for sure,
This vibrant life is a laughably pure.

So wander down paths where giggles arise,
For nature here wears no serious disguise.
With each little stumble and playful roar,
Life in the woods is never a bore.

Flickers of Gold Among the Firs

In the heart where sunlight plays hide and seek,
Gold flickers dancing, cheeky and sleek.
Bugs in a conga line wiggle and sway,
While grumpy old trees shout 'Get off my bay!'.

Beneath a fir, shadows loom like ghosts,
Little animals gather, they always boast.
"Who can hop highest?" they giggle and cheer,
While a wise old owl just shakes his rear.

A woodpecker drums, holding his beat,
As squirrels hold championships using their feet.
Nature's a circus with laughs all around,
Where the humor of flora and fauna is found.

So come take a stroll, see the snippets of fun,
Under boughs where giggles and gold ever run.
In the flickers of light, the joy isn't small,
Where life is a jest, and we're blessed with it all.

Sylvan Moments of Stillness

Amidst the leaves, a squirrel prances,
Chasing shadows, taking chances.
A chipmunk giggles, hiding snacks,
While birds debate the latest facts.

The trees sway gently, whispering jokes,
As fungi dance like woodland folks.
The sun peeks in with a golden grin,
While rabbits burst forth, their antics begin.

A breeze tickles branches, makes them sway,
The forest laughs in its own way.
A deer trips lightly on a hidden root,
While bees hum tunes in their wooden suit.

In this strange realm of furry and fine,
Every critter knows how to play divine.
With nature's humor filling the air,
It's impossible not to stop and stare.

The Velvet Nest of Nature

In the nest, a robin knits,
Threads of twigs in feathery bits.
The wind jests, pulls at her hat,
She squawks, 'Hey! I'm busy! How about that?'

A picnic set for ants so sly,
They bring their food and wave goodbye.
A party of frogs croaks, 'Dance with me!'
While a snail brings chips and raspberry tea.

A fox wanders in, looking quite suave,
But trip on a branch, oh what a laugh!
His friends all holler, "Try not to fall!"
Echoes burst out, a woodland call.

The sun yawns wide, casting a glow,
As creatures settle for the evening show.
With crickets chirping their nightly tune,
The velvet nest croons beneath the moon.

A Journey through Moss-Kissed Shadows

Through shadows where the mushrooms twirl,
A caterpillar dons a twinkly pearl.
He wobbles forth, proud and bold,
But steps on a leaf, and oh, behold!

The forest giggles with each stumble,
As hedgehogs snicker, their spines all rumble.
A raccoon claps, for this is the show,
While fireflies dance, all aglow.

A wise old owl chuckles on high,
Saying, "Young ones, give it a try!"
With mossy paths that twist and bend,
Every step, a giggle, a new blend.

In these shaded nooks, the laughter grows,
As woodland creatures share their woes.
One misstep leads to another flurry,
Yet still they stroll, never in a hurry.

The Essence of Dappled Light

Dappled beams through the branches play,
Casting patterns that dance and sway.
A squirrel pirouettes on a strand,
While shadows giggle, so soft and grand.

The flowers whisper, 'Look at me!'
As a bee tumbles from tree to tree.
A funny hat made of daisy lace,
Even the wind can't keep a straight face.

Chasing sunlight, the rabbits race,
With floppy ears, they pick up pace.
A turtle sighs, "Just take your time!"
While froggies croak a new nursery rhyme.

In the dappled light, the laughter swells,
Nature tells secrets that no one sells.
As twilight settles, the smiles remain,
In this joyful realm, we feel no pain.

Murmurs from the Heart of the Forest

In the woods where squirrels prance,
Trees hold secrets, a funny dance.
Rabbits giggle, leaves do sway,
Whispering jokes in a leafy ballet.

Frogs croak out a wild old song,
While owls hoot, but not for long.
Each branch sways with a chuckle loud,
Nature's laughter, both bright and proud.

A deer trips over a root so neat,
Lost in thoughts, it stumbles on its feet.
The sun peeks through, a playful tease,
Shining down on all with ease.

So walk with joy, let worries cease,
As the forest's humor grants you peace.
With every step on this fun parade,
Let your heart be light in the wild cascade.

The Solitary Symphony

In a glade where trees stand still,
A lone beetle climbs up the hill.
It plays a tune on a tiny shell,
As crickets join in with a cheerful yell.

Leaves clap hands in the gentle breeze,
Joining the chorus as they tease.
A turtle grins, it moves so slow,
It's the star of the show, don't you know?

Watch the raccoons, oh so sly,
Juggling acorns as they fly.
Laughter echoes through the green,
The forest's giggle, rarely seen.

So hum along with this woodland band,
With every note, take a stand.
For in this place where odd hearts meet,
Life sings a tune that's wild and sweet.

A Journey into the Green Stillness

In the green where shadows blend,
A caterpillar makes a new friend.
It tickles the ferns, oh what a sight,
With laughter that dances into the night.

Moss-covered stones, they start to laugh,
As the brook tells tales of the forest's half.
The bumblebees buzz a silly tune,
While daisies sway beneath the moon.

A fox trots by in a jaunty cap,
Saying, 'Life's a joke, take a nap!'
Toads leap high, in comic flair,
Filling the air with blissful air.

So skip along on this merry quest,
Nature's punchline is the very best.
For in this stillness, joy is found,
Laughter echoes all around.

The Embrace of Sylvan Silence

In a realm where silence reigns,
A porcupine plots with tiny gains.
It juggles twigs, quite a strange sight,
With spines that twinkle in soft light.

A bush rustles, what's that sound?
A raccoon stuck, it's homeward bound!
With plucky charm and a gentle grin,
It dances back with a clumsy spin.

Trees exchange tales in the hush so sweet,
Of runaway shoes and lost pet feet.
Breezes giggle, teasing the air,
As nature's whispers float without a care.

So pause awhile in this playful space,
With every moment, share your grace.
For life is funny, wrapped in green,
Where joy and laughter can often be seen.

Reflections in the Woodland Mirror

In the woods, with a grin wide,
Squirrels play hide, it's quite a ride.
Trees huddle close, whispering jokes,
While owls roll their eyes at silly folks.

A deer prances by, with a jaunty flair,
Wearing a crown made of leafy hair.
A chipmunk chuckles, offering tea,
"Care for a laugh? Join us, and see!"

Beneath the arch of branches green,
Frogs jump and croak, a funny scene.
Nature's own stand-up, wild and free,
In the woodland mirror, who could disagree?

With each rustle, a punchline springs,
Laughter erupts, oh how it sings.
Nature's comedy, wild and pure,
Come join the fun, it's a woodland tour!

Embracing the Green Stillness

In the heart of green, where we lay low,
Grass tickles toes, which makes you glow.
With a squirrel's twitch, the calm aligns,
Laughter bubbles up like sunshine shines.

A tree stands tall, with branches wide,
A raccoon sneaks in for a joyride.
Hey, watch your step, don't trip or fall,
The mossy floor is softer than all!

The sun winks down, playful and bright,
Casting shadows that dance with delight.
Even the breeze joins in the fun,
Who knew stillness could be this run?

So here we stay, in giggles and glee,
Nature's embrace, a wild jamboree.
With whispers of leaves and laughter blend,
This green stillness, the best of friends!

Steps on a Mossy Carpet

On a soft carpet of nature's green,
Every step feels like bouncing on a bean.
Moss cushions toes in a comical way,
With mushrooms standing guard, come join the play!

In this trodden path of giggles and sighs,
Crickets chirp jokes; who can deny?
Each footfall springs laughter like springs,
As bushes chuckle, oh what funny things!

The sun peeks through with a playful ray,
While rabbits hop, causing a ballet.
Birds wink and tweet, in a pitch just right,
Who knew the woods would be such a sight?

So tread with a grin, let laughter flow,
Each squishy step steals the show.
In this forest stage, joyfully taking part,
Every mossy stride is a dance from the heart!

Dreams Weaved in Woodland Shadows

In shadows deep, where secrets hide,
A badger dreams with a snoozing pride.
Unfurling dreams of carrot delight,
While fireflies giggle in the warm moonlight.

A clever fox paints tales in the air,
While frogs gossip without a care.
The night sky twinkles, oh what a scene,
Crafted by laughter, if only we glean.

The owls, wise, wear spectacles tight,
Mulling over jokes till the dawn's light.
"What do leaves say when they fall down?"
Why, nothing at all, they just clown around!

So here we drift in this shadowy play,
Where woodland dreams have much to say.
Laughter and whispers weave through the night,
In these lovely woods, everything feels right!

Stillness in the Forest Breath

Trees are tall and oh so proud,
Whisper to the clouds, aloud.
Squirrels dance in a funny way,
Taking nuts for their ballet.

A snail zooms by, a speedster rare,
On his shell, he grows a chair.
Birds gossip like they're in a café,
Sharing secrets of the day.

Roots entangle, a tangle in sight,
Fungi giggle in dim moonlight.
Moss joins the party, feeling grand,
Creating cushions where dreams land.

Nature grins, it's quite the tease,
A breeze tickles with perfect ease.
Life together, a funny blend,
In this forest where giggles never end.

Nature's Quiet Embrace

In a glade, a friendly frog,
Croaks his tales, a sage-like log.
Butterflies argue, with painted wings,
Who's the best at flapping swings?

A fox slips by, in stylish coat,
He stops to strut, the forest's goat.
Mushrooms snicker, all in a row,
"This spot's the best, don't you know?"

Sunbeams waltz through branches bold,
Dancing shadows that never get old.
A ladybug with a crown of spots,
Commands the daisies, "Hey, give me lots!"

Whispers of laughter in every nook,
Twirling in rhythms of nature's book.
In this realm of soft, warm hugs,
Every creature feels the love that chugs.

Shelter of Silent Pines

Tall and quirky, the pines stand still,
Hiding secrets, yet bringing thrill.
Underneath, a family of ants,
Practices their marches, doing happy dances.

A woodpecker taps like a barbell pro,
Each knock a joke, a friendly show.
Owls wear glasses, wise and clear,
Contemplating over targets—"Dinner near?"

The shadows stretch, a comedic play,
As rabbits hop in their silly ballet.
Chipmunks clad in striped pajamas,
Panic at the sight of a stray banana.

Even the stones chuckle low,
As toadstools bounce like they're in a show.
In this shelter, laughter signs,
Fill the air, amidst the pines.

Meditative Amongst the Maples

Maple leaves swirl in a sweet old chase,
Twisting and turning, a wobbly race.
Raccoons watch, tip-of-the-nose,
Wondering where all the laughter goes.

A hare takes time for a yoga stretch,
While a beetle plots a tiny sketch.
Branches sway as if to say,
"Chill out, friends, this is our day!"

Squirrels debate about the best nut,
"Cashew's the champ!" shouts a slow-strutting mutt.
The air is thick with laughter and fun,
Where nature dances, we all are one.

So come and bask in the humor benign,
Under these branches, everything's fine.
In this timeless zone of quiet mirth,
You'll find the joy that fills the earth.

A Reverie Amidst the Pines

In the woods where squirrels play,
I tripped on roots and lost my way.
A chipmunk chuckled, filled with cheer,
"Do you need a map, my dear?"

The trees all sighed, a gentle flock,
As I danced around a fallen rock.
A fungus said, "Join in the fun!"
We laughed till the setting sun.

A rabbit winked, said, "What a mess!"
I grinned back, feeling quite blessed.
Nature hosts a silly ball,
Where every creature joins the call.

In the green, the laughter spread,
With all the critters, joy instead.
Pine needles whisper funny tales,
And life here never ever fails.

Echoes of Yesterday in the Woodlands

Forest echoes, a quirky sound,
As I wander, round and round.
A fox in glasses gave a wink,
"Lost again? Just take a drink!"

The trees are gossips, wild and free,
Whispering secrets, just to me.
A woodpecker with a tiny hat,
Said, "Watch your head, beware the spat!"

Underneath a mushroom's shade,
A ladybug got laid and played.
She laughed and spun, a tiny queen,
In this realm where life's a dream.

As the leaves began to shake,
A troupe of ants danced by the lake.
"Come join us!" they shouted, full of glee,
In this funny place, I'm finally free!

Veils of Mist and Memory

Misty morning, oh what a sight,
A snail raced by, in sheer delight.
He challenged me, a sprinting game,
But I just watched and called his name.

The fog, a blanket, draped the trees,
I sneezed aloud, forgetting the breeze.
An owl hooted, wearing a frown,
"Not now, buddy, let's not clown!"

Each step echoes with giggles galore,
As raccoons plot a friendly score.
"Who's who?" squeaked lost little chip,
In this comedy, we all just trip!

In the mist, memories swirl and dance,
With every critter, a second chance.
A funny world, beneath the dew,
Where laughter grows like morning blooms.

The Lullaby of Dappled Light

Beneath the leaves, the shadows play,
Sunbeams wiggle, all day, hooray!
A caterpillar sang a tune,
"Scoot over! I want this afternoon!"

In dappled light, we found a spree,
Where giggles rolled like waves in the sea.
A butterfly, dressed in stripes,
Sipped nectar while sharing gripes.

A gentle breeze whispered jokes, so sly,
I clutched my belly and nearly cried.
"Why did the tree go to class?"
"To improve its photosynthes-'gas'!"

As the sun dipped low behind the trees,
Nature chuckled, swayed with ease.
In every corner, joy takes flight,
In this place, laughter feels so right!

Mossy Paths of Quietude

Along the mossy paths I roam,
Where squirrels plot and gnomes call home.
The mushrooms giggle, oh what a sight,
Whispering secrets in the fading light.

A hedgehog winks, quite proud of his spines,
While rabbits wear hats made of twines.
The trees are gossiping, branches a-flap,
As I trip over roots, taking a nap.

Fungi in slippers, dancing so free,
I'm certain they're laughing, just wait and see.
With every step, the ground does chuckle,
In this woodsy wonder, life's all a snuggle.

In this kingdom of green, where nonsense unfolds,
Dreams are woven in fibrous gold.
So join the ballet of leaves and of bark,
And let your heart soar, igniting a spark.

Shadows Dance in the Glade

In the glade where shadows tease,
The trees sway gently with playful ease.
The sun tickles leaves with a golden stare,
While critters gawk and sigh in the air.

A raccoon tries to juggle some nuts,
With little success, oh, what a strut!
The birds gossip high on branches so sweet,
Gossiping loudly of the raccoons' defeat.

Beneath the floor of a leafy embrace,
The worms hold a party, keep up with the pace!
They wiggle and jiggle, whilst dancers spin round,
In this bizarre jamboree, laughter resounds.

As twilight falls, a firefly's glow,
Turns the far edge of chaos to a soft show.
So step in the glade, take laughter's sweet hand,
And dance with the shadows, let fun be your brand.

Harmony in the Rustic Air

In the air that's thick with earthy surprise,
The bees are the band, buzzing harmonized.
With butterflies twirling in a wobbly flight,
It's a concert of critters every day and night.

Chipmunks in shades play a trumpet so grand,
While owls in tuxedos lend a helping hand.
Grasshoppers leap, in a jazzy delight,
In the rustic amphitheater under moonlight.

The wind plays a tune, tucked in tree bends,
Blowing tickles from roots to the ends.
Chortling owls hoot as they play the sly game,
It's a symphony of mischief, never the same.

So clap for the band in this leafy retreat,
Where laughter and music make life so sweet.
Join in the chorus, don't be shy,
In the woods' merry hall, let your spirits fly!

The Silent Watcher of the Woods

A wise old owl, perched high, does grin,
With spectacles perched upon its chin.
It watches the antics of creatures below,
From way up high, where the breezes flow.

Squirrels race down, a competition of sorts,
While frogs throw parties with rambunctious cohorts.
The owl just chuckles, tilting its head,
As the madness unfolds in the forest bed.

The raccoons are sneaking a snack from a pot,
But the pot's been guarded, oh what a plot!
With paws in a whirl, they tip and they flop,
While the owl just hoots, "Oh, please never stop!"

As night drapes down and the moon starts to gleam,
The woods are alive, it's a wild, funny dream.
The silent observer, wise, quirky, and bold,
Guards the enchantment, let the tales unfold.

The Ballet of the Falling Leaves

Leaves swirl and twirl, in a dizzying dance,
Flipping for squirrels, they take quite a chance.
Whirling like dancers, they plummet with glee,
Nature's own ballet, come join the spree!

The trees laugh and wiggle, a rustling cheer,
As acorns roll down, it's the time of the year.
With crickets providing a tune in the breeze,
It's a grand show to watch, oh, if you please!

But wait! What's that sound? A thud on my head!
An acorn had plummeted, straight from its bed!
The trees burst with laughter, as I rub my crown,
Guess life in the forest is full of let-downs!

So come, take a seat on this leafy tableau,
Where seasons conspire and time moves so slow.
Nature's ticklish moments, oh how they tease,
In this merry show, there's nothing to freeze!

Nature's Quiet Canvas

In this forest of colors, the palette is grand,
With trunks in deep brown and leaves ginger-sand.
Critters paint laughter with every small leap,
Creating a canvas where silence can't sleep.

A bird, all in blue, forgets how to sing,
Dances on branches, it's quite the wild thing!
A fox in a tuxedo struts with charm and flair,
While the rascally raccoons steal snacks from mid-air.

Sunlight spills gold, as the shadows parade,
Each rustle, a giggle, in the forest's charade.
With giggles and snickers, the leaves play the part,
Nature's own jesters, all masters of art!

So grab your painted brush, let's blend every hue,
And sketch silly tales where the wildlife renew.
In this tranquil retreat, let hilarity flow,
For laughter's the secret in nature's tableau!

Hushed Lullabies of the Trees

Whispering winds weave through branches that sway,
The trees hum a tune, oh so far away.
A symphony stirs, in the hush of the night,
Marshmallows dance while fireflies take flight.

Bunnies hop softly, they sway to the beat,
While owls, with their wisdom, quietly tweet.
The crickets are playing their tiny guitars,
Making night's music, beneath the bright stars.

But watch out for raccoons, they're plotting a play,
In moonlight, they skitter, all fun and cliché.
With masks made of mischief, they cause such a fuss,
Creating a ruckus, oh, what a plus!

So close your eyes tight, let the night gently tease,
As the lullabies carry on the soft breeze.
In nature's embrace, let your dreams take flight,
With critters as witnesses, throughout the night!

A Reverie Beneath the Branches

Under canopies leafy, where shadows grow thick,
I ponder the vine that I call my old stick.
The squirrels play charades, stealing cones from the sky,
While turtles in slow-mo, just watch and comply.

A rabbit in slippers hops high and low,
Sipping on dew drops, oh how they flow!
The fungi are laughing, in colors so bright,
While ants march like soldiers, all in a line fight.

The air fills with giggles, it's hard not to smile,
Though I trip on an acorn and stumble a mile.
The trees shake their branches, they chuckle and sway,
In nature's own concert, we dance and we play!

So sit back and enjoy, with friends all around,
In the realm of the green, such joy can be found.
Beneath lofty branches, where laughter takes flight,
This reverie delights, in the day and the night!

A Harvest of Tranquil Thoughts

In the woods where squirrels dance,
And chipmunks steal a glance,
I ponder life while gnawing bark,
On benches made from trees so dark.

Leaves gossip lightly, in a breeze,
As bugs hold court upon the trees,
I chuckle at a crow's debate,
On who has found the best nut fate.

The frogs croak jokes in the pond,
While bees try hard to abscond,
A game of tag among the weeds,
A laugh erupts, a sprout then leads.

Nature's jesters, quite a crew,
With laughter mixed in morning dew,
So let us dance, be light and spry,
In the forest, under the sky.

Embraced by Nature's Whisper

An owl hoots, he's quite the sage,
His wisdom penned on every page,
I nod along, in leafy chairs,
While trees show off their quirky hairs.

A bunny hops, with great finesse,
In a waistcoat made of grass no less,
I chuckle hard, what style he wears,
To dine on clover, if he dares.

The creek gurgles in a playful tone,
As sunbeams make the shadows moan,
A squirrel's acorn, a bouncing prize,
He hides it well, or so he tries.

With every rustle, laughter weaves,
Through tangled roots and fallen leaves,
Here in this jesting leafy den,
Nature's charm calls us once again.

The Dusk of Woodland Rest

When evening drapes its velvet cloak,
The fireflies gossip, giggle and poke,
Stars peek out like tiny eyes,
Observing us in our woodland guise.

The raccoon, slick in a stylish hat,
Claims treasure maps but why? Who knows that?
He munches snacks with a thieving grin,
Stealing cookies from the picnic bin.

Twilight giggles, crickets sing,
As trees unfold their nightly fling,
A woodpecker taps, keeping the beat,
While sleepy deer find their chance to eat.

Nature whispers, "Join the fun!"
In the woodlands, we're never done,
This laughter lingers in the air,
As we sway and share without a care.

An Oasis of Rustic Calm

Here in a clearing, time stands still,
With laughter ringing, a joyous thrill,
Sun-kissed laughter in every ray,
As rabbits play hide and seek all day.

Wooden swings, swaying side to side,
In this lush land, let joy reside,
A bear does a jig, quite out of tune,
Underneath the smiling moon.

Each blossom dances with a twirl,
As ladybugs have their daily whirl,
Squirrels stash nuts, and giggle aloud,
In their nutty game, they're quite proud.

The brook chuckles, a bubbling song,
In this haven, we all belong,
So let's toast to the fun we found,
In nature's peace, so silly and sound.

Fables of the Forest Floor

Once a squirrel wore a hat,
He thought he looked quite fat.
But slipped on acorns, oh dear!
He tumbled over, full of cheer.

A wise old owl said with a hoot,
"Squirrels don't wear silly loot!"
But the squirrel just laughed, "Oh please,
I'm the king of this nutty tease!"

The mushroom danced, it took a chance,
While ants all joined in a prance.
They twirled 'round ferns, a wild show,
Under the sun's warm, golden glow.

A rabbit joined with leaps and bounds,
As laughter rang through leafy sounds.
Together they spun tales of old,
In the forest's embrace, brave and bold.

Secrets in the Twisted Roots

In tangled roots, a secret lay,
A gnome snoozed through the sunny day.
His dreams involved a carrot feast,
With dancing veggies, quite the beast.

A hedgehog poked his head around,
And whispered, "Gnome! There's joy abound!"
But the gnome just snored with glee,
"Who needs the world? Just let me be!"

The mushrooms giggled, sharing tales,
Of gnomes and their amusing fails.
A wiry fox crept up with sass,
Tripped on roots and fell with class.

The sun set low, casting gold,
As forest dwellers, brave and bold,
Shared stories 'neath the twinkling stars,
In laughter, life's funny memoirs.

An Ode to the Leafy Canopy

Up in the trees, the branches sway,
Where birds chirp songs all through the day.
One parrot thought he was a star,
Singing off-key, loud from afar.

A squirrel tried to join the band,
With maracas made of pine cone hand.
But all he did was shake and shiver,
Until he fell, oh what a quiver!

A breeze came through, it laughed and joked,
While tree trunks swayed, all twigs provoked.
The leaves rustled in gentle ridicule,
As if to say, "You're such a fool!"

But up above, all was quite grand,
With sun-kissed leaves that took a stand.
In this leafy realm, joy took flight,
Making even the birds giggle with delight.

The Quietude of Pine Needles

In the dense woods where pine needles lay,
A raccoon thought he'd bake a soufflé.
But with paws as clumsy as a shoe,
He tossed the mix, and bam! It flew!

The pine trees chuckled, oh so tall,
As the raccoon tripped and began to sprawl.
"Cooking's not for furry paws!"
He muttered back while holding jaws.

A wise old tortoise crept on by,
With a shell that glimmered in the sky.
"Why not eat nuts instead of bake?"
He said with a grin, oh for goodness' sake!

The forest giggled at the mess,
Pine needles cloaked the raccoon's stress.
In the quietude, humor took shape,
As woodland antics added a grape!

Nature's Bounty of Stillness

Beneath the trees, a squirrel prances,
Chasing shadows, doing funny dances.
Mushrooms giggle, they all know well,
Secrets of the woods, they seldom tell.

A rabbit laughs, with ears so long,
Jumping about, all day, feeling strong.
The sunlight tickles the leaves so bright,
While crickets chirp, in pure delight.

A bear in shades, taking a nap,
Dreaming of honey and maybe a map.
A wise owl hoots, "What's all the fuss?"
Trees chuckle softly, "Just wait for us."

With silent waves of the breeze nearby,
Nature's laughter echoes, oh my!
In this realm where joy can sprout,
Even the mushrooms have fun, no doubt!

Sighs of the Whispering Pines

Whispering pines, with laughter they sigh,
Sharing tall tales of birds zooming by.
The mushrooms below, burst into cheers,
As squirrels throw acorns like frisbees, my dears!

A porcupine prances, with style and grace,
Although a few thorns are out of place.
Branches above giggle, swaying around,
While critters assemble with merry sound.

A raccoon juggles, just using his paws,
Chasing his tail, with roars of applause.
The logs chuckle with ample delight,
As twilight brings fireflies, flashing bright.

Under moonlight, the laughter won't cease,
Nature's pranks fill the night with ease.
In a world where silliness reigns supreme,
Even the forest knows how to dream!

The Peace Beneath the Boughs

Under boughs, a gopher plays hide and seek,
While a sleepy turtle lies down for a peek.
A songbird croons, with a wink in its eye,
"Come join the fun, it's not a badbye!"

Despite their trouble, a fox sneezes loud,
Alerting the deer, who joins in the crowd.
Oaks whisper jokes, as the squirrels attend,
With laughter that pops, like a fizzy blend!

A bumblebee buzzes, wearing a crown,
Sipping sweet nectar, spinning around.
A fish in a pond, just looking to float,
Spots a frog, who claims its new coat!

Beneath leafy treasures, where silliness grows,
Nature laughs lightly, as everyone knows.
Here, peace reigns with a spark of fun,
Amid the woodlands, there's joy to be spun!

Shadows that Shape the Earth

Shadows dance lightly, under the moon,
While owls tell tales, making time swoon.
Rabbits in capes, playing trick or treat,
Hop to the rhythm, oh isn't it sweet?

A branch that's a bellyache, chuckles awry,
Tickled by breezes that drift softly by.
Fungi in hats, sitting quite still,
Snickering softly, holding their thrill.

Waves of laughter from streams so bright,
Where fishes in clowns' wigs swim with delight.
A snail in a race, oh what a sight,
Where slow wins the prize, what a clever plight!

So here in the shadows, where goofballs play,
The earth shapes a poem, in its own funny way.
Under the whispers and giggles we find,
Nature's fine humor, forever aligned!

Serenity Among the Tall Pines

In the woods where squirrels play,
Gentle whispers hold their sway.
Trees giggle with a creaky sound,
As pines catch laughter all around.

A chair made of branches so fine,
Sits idle, sipping on some brine.
A squirrel wears a leafy crown,
While the owl jests from his high throne.

Birds gossip in the leafy halls,
Echoing jokes through the tree's tall walls.
The breeze tells tales both silly and grand,
As nature's jesters make their stand.

Sunset brings a comical sight,
As shadows dance with pure delight.
With wings unfurled, the bugs all dance,
In the pines, where they take a chance.

Echoes of the Woodland Breeze

The wind chuckles through the leaves,
In the forest where humor weaves.
Branches sway as if to tease,
While critters gather down by the knees.

A fox sneezes, and everyone stares,
As squirrels giggle, trading glares.
Nature's laughter echoes loud,
Making even shy deer feel proud.

Clouds drift by with a comic twist,
Creating shapes that can't be missed.
A moose in glasses reads a map,
While birds in hats prepare for a nap.

Under the canopy where laughter rains,
Life is light, free from chains.
In the woodland's whispering spree,
Joy is found in pure folly.

The Stillness of Cedar Dreams

Cedar trees share winks at dusk,
Their branches sway with playful musk.
Bugs on stilts do a little jig,
While a chubby bear eats a twig.

In slumber's grasp, a fox might grin,
While dreams of ham dance in his skin.
Owls in tuxedos hoot in delight,
As night unfolds with silent might.

Moonbugs sporting tiny hats,
Read poetry to chirpy rats.
Stars twinkle with a knowing nod,
As the world chuckles, blissfully flawed.

In dreams where silence plays its tune,
Nature's whimsy makes us swoon.
Cedar serenades, oh so mellow,
Wrap us tight, like a soft pillow.

Sunlight through Leafy Veils

Sunbeams sneak through leafy doors,
   Creating patterns on the floors.
   A rabbit in shades takes a seat,
  As the sun tickles his furry feet.

The leaves dance in a goofy parade,
   While shadows play, unafraid.
  A chipmunk wearing a little bow tie,
   Gives a salute as he walks by.

Laughter clings to the golden rays,
  As light tickles in bizarre ways.
  A bear tries to juggle his lunch,
While squirrels gather for a munch.

In this spectacle of nature's glee,
  Even the mosses seem to agree.
Sunshine whispers, "Have some fun,"
  As the day melts into the run.

A Tapestry of Green

In the woods where gnomes reside,
Squirrels bicker, tails all wide.
Laughter echoes through the pines,
As nature dances, bold designs.

A raccoon wearing fancy hats,
Juggles acorns with the bats.
Birds sing songs off-key, oh dear,
The trees just chuckle, never fear.

Mushrooms sport their polka dots,
While rabbits strategize their plots.
Beneath the shade, a picnic scene,
Peanut butter—extra green!

As shadows stretch, the sun sets low,
A fox attempts a stand-up show.
Laughter ripples through the night,
In this wood, all feels just right.

The Sapling's Soliloquy

A little sprout stood proud today,
"Why can't I grow like trees?" it said.
With branches high and leaves so wide,
It dreamed of heights, a leafy bed.

The old oak chuckled with a grin,
"Patience, pal, don't rush your scene!
You'll stretch and reach, just like your kin,
With roots so deep and leaves of green."

Nearby, a fox stole all the show,
Dancing 'neath the sunny glow.
"Why try to grow? Just learn to sway!
Join in the fun, it's a great play!"

The sapling sighed, it found great cheer,
To laugh and dance without a fear.
So up it reached, but with a twist—
It learned that joy can coexist.

Still Waters in the Forest's Heart

By the pond where ducklings swim,
A frog joins in to sing a hymn.
With croaks and splashes all around,
Each ripple carries joy profound.

A turtle in a hat quite tall,
Waves to friends, then has a ball.
He flips and flops, such silly moves,
Each splash inspires wild grooves.

The fish giggle as they dive,
In this pond, they feel alive.
With bubbles popping, what a sight!
A fishy dance in pure delight.

As twilight sets, the fireflies gleam,
Nature's quirks are the perfect theme.
In still waters, laughter sparkles bright,
As friends unite in pure delight.

Winding Trails of Solace

On a path where seedlings grow,
A platypus starts a show.
With waddles, slides, and quirks galore,
Every step opens a door.

A chipmunk yells, "Catch me if you dare!"
While bunnies bounce without a care.
The trail is filled with merry jest,
In this forest, we're truly blessed.

An owl looms, wise as can be,
"Minding your business? Come just see!
For trails may twist and turn just right,
Adventure awaits in morning light."

With chattering friends, they roam around,
Each corner brings a new sound.
In the heart where laughter calls,
Winding trails show fun for all.

A Reverent Walk Among Giants

In the forest deep, where the tall ones rise,
Many birds squawk loud, and squirrels disguise.
I tiptoe past trunks, my eyes wide and bright,
Wondering if trees ever giggle at night.

They whisper sweet secrets, woodsy and grand,
With wise, knotted fingers, they wave their hand.
I laugh at their roots, so tangled and spry,
Do legs grow out of bark, or do they just sigh?

As I roam the aisles of this leafy old shop,
A deer prances by, then does an odd hop.
It's a dance with the flora, a shuffle, a swirl,
In the land of the giants, where dreams start to twirl.

So I strut with the shadows, my heart feels so light,
Amid laughter of boughs, life's comedy takes flight.
Nature's a joker with jokes hard to beat,
Each step my own punchline, so funny, so sweet.

Swaying Limbs and Silent Thoughts

The leaves are a-whispering in playful delight,
Branches sway softly, a delightful sight.
I ponder if trees have a rhythm to hum,
Or would they just chuckle and say, "Here we come!"

With limbs like mischief, they stretch toward the sky,
As if reaching for clouds, not a single goodbye.
I scowl at a branch that tickles my chin,
Is it friendly or feisty, where to begin?

I invite the sun's gleam to dance on my face,
The wind joins the party, causing a race.
With every gust blowing, the humor rings clear,
Why do the ferns laugh? They've had too much cheer!

In this grove, all my thoughts can sway and delight,
Nature's a jester, and I'm feeling just right.
With chortles of squirrels as my whimsical guide,
Among swaying limbs, I find giggles and glide.

Where the Ferns Repose

In a patch of green, where ferns play coy,
They whisper of secrets, with nature's own joy.
Taking a break from their leafy charade,
Do they dream of dances or simply parade?

Each curl holds a giggle, each leaf a soft grin,
Where do they go, when the sun starts to spin?
In shadows, they chuckle, avoid the sun's beam,
Plotting their pranks like a team in a dream.

A pogo-stick rabbit hops by with a thump,
Ferns burst into laughter, the whole world a jump.
With each little flutter, I join in the fun,
Nature's a playground, and ho, what a run!

So here in this haven, with giggles that soar,
I dip and I twirl on the moss-covered floor.
The ferns and I chuckle, a whimsical team,
In a world full of wonders, let's live out the dream.

The Soft Glow of a Wooden Dawn

As dawn peeks shyly through branches entwined,
A sleepy old log greets me, unrefined.
With a yawn of the forest, the day starts to sip,
While ants in the grass hold a breakfast trip.

The sunlight tickles the bark of the trees,
I chuckle at shadows as they shimmy with ease.
A woodpecker's drumbeat joins in with a flair,
Who knew morning's concert could be such a scare?

With laughter from leaves, and a breeze oh-so-fine,
How do trees smile? They bend and they twine.
Each knot tells a story, of giggles and glee,
In every nook and cranny, the humor's the key.

So I sit on this log, as the bright sun shines on,
In the glow of the morning, I join in the fun.
The world's just a joke with each twist and each bend,
In this wooden abode, where all paths seem to blend.

The Gentle Touch of Sunlight

Beneath the boughs, I squint and grin,
A squirrel darts by, it's quite the win.
The sunlight tickles like a feathered tease,
I laugh so hard, I stumble on my knees.

A chubby bunny munches on a leaf,
His nibbling sound, a comic relief.
Bright beams of gold dance on my cheek,
Nature's giggles play hide and seek.

A butterfly lands, a tiny seat,
I wave with glee, isn't life sweet?
With every rustle, my worries fade,
In this sunny spot, I'm perfectly paid.

So here I lounge, with laughter loud,
Amongst the trees, I'm feeling proud.
Nature's humor, a joyous gift,
With every glance, my spirit lifts.

Resting in Nature's Heart

On a mossy bed, I take a nap,
Dreams of squirrels in a silly cap.
The breeze whispers jokes, oh so clever,
I chuckle so hard, my nap's gone forever.

A raccoon peeks, with a curious eye,
I wave hello, he looks awry.
He shuffles away, with a snack in tow,
It's a critter's feast, don't you know?

The sun dips low, casting shadows tall,
My resting spot feels like a ball.
With every chirp, the world arrives,
In nature's heart, hilarity thrives.

I tip my hat to the buzzing bee,
He buzzes back, "Stay away from me!"
In this wild place, where laughter's free,
I've found my joy, just being me.

The Language of Rustling Boughs

The branches chat, with creaks and groans,
Sharing tales in their woody tones.
A playful wind joins in the fun,
Tickling leaves 'til day is done.

The squirrels gossip with tiny squeaks,
All while I study their fruity peaks.
"Hey, look at that!" the oak tree said,
"It's just a human, munching bread!"

The whispers grow, it's quite absurd,
A chorus of laughter, without a word.
Each leaf shares a joke, it seems,
As I chuckle along in daydreams.

So I sit back, with nature's cheer,
In this comedy show, I find myself near.
Among the whispers, I take my part,
In the language of trees, that warms the heart.

Whispers of the Earth

The ground below hums a funny tune,
A mole pops up, but it's out of tune.
He wiggles his nose, looks quite confused,
In this earthy world, I've found my muse.

The flowers gossip, they sway and preen,
"Did you see her hat? It's really keen!"
While ants march by in a tiny parade,
All in good humor, in sunlight's shade.

I catch a glimpse of a dandy beetle,
Dressed to impress, oh what a steeple!
He struts his stuff like a runway star,
In this whimsical world, how bizarre!

So I'll laugh with the leaves, and dance with the bees,
In this merry place where I'm free to please.
With whispers of earth, I find delight,
In this joyous realm, everything feels right.

The Song of the Old Oak

Old Oak stood tall, with quite a grin,
Swaying to the wind, doing a spin.
His acorns drop, a goofy little dance,
Each one a hat, giving squirrels a chance.

Branches like arms, he waves at the sun,
Tickling the clouds, oh what silly fun!
With birds in his hair, a real feathered show,
Old Oak laughs loudly, 'Hey, look at me grow!'

Breath of the Undergrowth

In the shadows where the critters play,
A chorus of giggles runs wild every day.
Frogs leaping high with croaks that sound sweet,
While ants wear sunglasses, they dance on their feet.

Mice hold a banquet, cheese all around,
They toast to the mushrooms, oh what a sound!
With worms as the band, they wiggle and jive,
Life in the brush — oh, it's quite the vibe!

A Lullaby of Fallen Leaves

Leaves fall like feathers, a colorful rain,
They whisper, 'Don't worry, we'll do this again!'
With crunches and giggles underfoot so loud,
Squirrels throw parties — aren't they quite proud?

Dancing in piles, they all take a dive,
'Catch me if you can!' says a leaf, oh so sly.
The tune of the tumble, a rustling cheer,
While the wind plays the harp, we all lend an ear!

In the Shade of the Elder Tree

Elder Tree chuckles, with wisdom so deep,
Telling tales of the roots, as the critters creep.
Rabbits in top hats, with tails quite absurd,
Debating the best way to hop like a bird.

Beneath every branch, there's laughter galore,
As hedgehogs debate on who can roll more.
Elder Tree nods, then starts to doze,
Wrapped in the fun, as the breeze gently blows.

The Lull of the Quiet Grove

In the grove, the squirrels sit,
Planning pranks, they think it's wit.
The trees roll eyes with leafy glee,
As acorns fall from bickering spree.

Chirping birds share silent jokes,
In branches high, they boast like folks.
The owls pretend to nap and yawn,
While raccoons steal away at dawn.

Rustling leaves lend echoes clear,
Of laughter that you almost hear.
A twig snaps loud, the laughter freeze,
A moment's pause, then bursts of tease.

In this place where whispers play,
The antics make the dull fade away.
With every chuckle, nature spins,
In the quiet grove, where joy begins.

Stillness at the Edge of the Thicket

At the thicket's edge, a dance unfolds,
Dancing critters, brave and bold.
The hedgehogs twist in quite a way,
While shy old rabbits watch the play.

A porcupine with puns so sharp,
Tells jokes that make the bushes harp.
Even the frogs croak out a song,
To join the fun, where all belong.

A breeze sweeps through and shakes a tree,
The laughter spills, it's wild and free.
Squirrels tumble, trip on roots,
While chipmunks strut in snazzy suits.

In this stillness, mischief brews,
As nature laughs, it's hard to snooze.
With every chuckle, spirits rise,
In the thicket's edge, beneath the skies.

Dreaming Under the Arched Branches

Under arches where shadows play,
Dreams of nuts in the light of day.
A badger snores with such a snort,
While ants parade with no retort.

The owls are wise, or so they say,
But last night's dinner led them astray.
A raccoon lost its tasty find,
While drowsy deer play hide and kind.

Branches creak like old folks tease,
As wind gives trees a joyful squeeze.
The whispers share their silly thoughts,
A mushroom giggles, learning dots.

Underneath the leafy seams,
Nature spins its quirky dreams.
With every snore, and every cheer,
The woods come alive with playful cheer.

A Serenade for the Woodland Spirits

A serenade in the woods so bright,
Woodland spirits take to flight.
Fairies dance on the tips of leaves,
While giggling owls weave their thieves.

Mice on stage with tiny hats,
Perform for the trees like acrobats.
Squirrels join in with little taps,
As nature claps with friendly snaps.

The brook sings along with splashes clear,
Echoing laughs that all can hear.
Even the rocks think they can groove,
In this enchanted spot, all move.

In every rustle, a tune's unfurled,
With joy and jest, they greet the world.
Each whisper in leaves keeps spirits near,
In this festive woodland atmosphere.

The Stillness of Earthbound Dreams

In a forest where squirrels play tricks,
A branch dances with shadows and kicks.
Roots gossip about the passing breeze,
While mushrooms wear hats, quite at ease.

Breezes whisper secrets to the trees,
They respond with a rustle, 'Oh, please!'
A snail boasts of his speedy retreat,
While ants march in formation on tiny feet.

The moon peeks through, a curious guest,
As crickets gather for a night's fest.
They chirp and they chirp, in their finest style,
Complaining about quiet for a while.

Yet in this wood where chaos is grace,
A frog makes faces, a comical place.
With nature's laughter in every stream,
Huey the owl captures wild dreams.

The Peaceful Grove at Dusk

In the grove, the trees start to share,
Whispered giggles float around in the air.
A raccoon plays tricks with apples so round,
While a squirrel throws acorns at the ground.

Beneath a sky brushed with fading light,
A rabbit sings ballads; oh, what a sight!
While owls blink slowly, sipping their tea,
Mice tap-dance for the bees, quite carefree.

The brook giggles softly, trickling near,
As frogs in tuxedos appear without fear.
They croak out jokes that only they get,
While all the fireflies begin to fret.

In this twilight nook, chaos feels right,
Where woodland mischief shines through the night.
There's a chuckle in the heart of each tree,
Nature's sweet humor is wild and free.

Dancing Blades of Grass

Blades of grass in the wind sway and sway,
Challenging each other to a dance play.
One claims he can moonwalk, another does spins,
While ladybugs judge from where the fun begins.

A worm pokes his head, says, 'Look at me go!'
He wriggles and jiggles; it's quite the show.
While butterflies flutter with their best moves,
Creating a rhythm that simply grooves.

The ants march in time, a formidable line,
With little top hats, they look so divine.
While bees buzz along in a chaotic beat,
Joining this dance, it's a feat quite complete.

In this grassy stage, joy leaps and bounds,
With critters and nature forming sweet sounds.
So when the sun sets, and the party's in full,
Every blade hosts a friend; it's never dull.

A Secret Haven of Calm

In a corner of woods, where whispers reside,
A turtlenecked turtle takes quite a stride.
He giggles as he slips on a leaf,
Creating a spectacle, beyond belief.

Nearby, the bushes gossip away,
Giving advice to the trees on display.
A fox in a scarf rolls down a hill,
While butterflies cheer, it's quite the thrill.

Blossoms laugh softly, as they sway in time,
With petals that twirl, oh so sublime.
The wind joins the fun, a tickle and tease,
While a sleepy old bear snoozes with ease.

In this haven, humor and nature entwine,
Each chuckle of branches a sweet little sign.
That laughter abounds, in this cozy glade,
Creating a world where joy's never swayed.